The **Better** Conversations RULEBOOK

A #1 Amazon Best Seller in Business
Management & Leadership (Top 100 Free)

The Better Conversations Rulebook is based on skills taught in the CPD Certified online course Leaders Who Coach™ that graduates are raving about, calling it *"transformational" "life-changing"* and *"brilliant"* consistently awarding it with 5 Star Ratings and 10/10 Net Promoter Scores.

Sehaam Cyrene is a leadership and team coach (PCC), creator of the Coach-Culture Team Map™ and Leaders Who Coach™. She advocates for leaders to step into the next era of leadership practice — to become coach-leaders.

https://betterconversations.co/sehaam-cyrene/

LinkedIn: @sehaam
Instagram: @TawKwrd

BETTER
CONVERSATIONS

+ Free
Mini
Course

The **Better** *Conversations* RULEBOOK

QUESTIONS & PHRASES
PRACTISED DAILY BY
Leaders Who Coach™

Sehaam Cyrene

The creator of the 5★ 10/10 NPS CPD Certified Course

THE
BETTER CONVERSATIONS
RULEBOOK

Questions & Phrases
Practised Daily by
Leaders Who Coach™

Sehaam Cyrene

First published 2023 by Better Conversations
& Associates Limited, UK

hello@betterconversations.co
https://BetterConversations.co/Rulebook/

ISBN: 9798854977654

*The Better Conversations Rulebook — Questions & Phrases
Practised Daily by Leaders Who Coach*™ is also available as an
ebook.

Edited by Sehaam Cyrene & Lizzie Daykin

*For Hali, Sophia and Kirk,
go shake the tree of life.
For my mum and my dad,
for showing me how.
For Linthur, aye.*

Many have contributed to who I am today by teaching me something or sharing time and space with me. Even in the toughest exchanges, I grew.

For hours of nourishing conversations, and for collaboration that never feels like work, thank you Lizzie Daykin, Heidi Cowie, Uschi Baumann, and of course Mag Leahy who trusted me enough and believes in the power of Leaders Who Coach™.

And to all the wonderful Leaders Who Coach™ and tutors on this journey who I continue to learn from. Without you, this would not exist. Thank you.

Contents

★ RULE #1 — EARN PERMISSION TO SPEAK

★ RULE #2 — TRUST UNDERPINS REPUTATION

★ RULE #3 — ZIP IT OR MISS IT

The Rulebook

No-one tells you what's really going on in a conversation. No-one explicitly signals that they're not listening to you, that they don't respect you, that you're sharing too much, or that your style of speaking shuts them down. Nor do they advise you that they're holding back valuable information, deprioritising the tasks you've delegated to them, or that they're trying to deceive or sabotage you.

The Better Conversations Rulebook uncovers the truth of what's happening, why some conversations play out in frustrating ways, and how *you* can transform them and your relationships at work.

Understand the rules of coach-leaders and you discover simple yet powerful ways to hold conversations that build trust, influence and reputation, encourage people to open up and share important ideas, and grow your confidence for the toughest conversations.

I've written The Rulebook to be easy to read, dip into often to tackle new challenges or refine your style, and use in your very next meeting. I reveal reliable coach-leadership strategies with 88 Questions & Phrases with clear explainers — wherever you see the ✦ symbol. This is what I teach Leaders Who Coach™ to use every day. My wish is for you to gain your human advantage in holding strong conversations with your direct reports, peers, suppliers and bosses.

The Better Conversations Rulebook is the wisdom you wish someone had placed firmly in your hands long ago. I know I do!

Welcome it now as your confidant and champion to becoming a coach-leader.

Leaders Who Coach™ have this magic of drawing people towards them. Except, it's not magic. They're just very intentional and strategic in how they connect with us, how they create emotional commitment in others, and how they build our confidence to do more with the skills and passions that we have. — Sehaam Cyrene

Coach-Leaders

Coach-Leaders are leaders who practise the skills of professional coaches for substantive impact — from one meeting to the next. For productivity, wellbeing, accountability, ownership, commitment, and growth.

The first thing to appreciate about coach-leaders is that they are always growing. This position invites learning, builds bridges and rewards them with wonderful, memorable conversations.

Coach-leaders consistently apply the skills of coaches to their conversations with colleagues. They notice and adjust the tempo based on what the other person needs, balancing it with the requirements of business.

Coach-leaders are a very special hybrid of coach and leader. They do not need to be certified or credentialed executive coaches. However, they do need training in the art of effective coach-leadership.

Here are some distinctions we observe about Leaders Who Coach™:

People & relationships are a priority

They are less busy with processes and tasks, or with fire-fighting and fixing. They get work done by empowering others.

Set strategy & delegate effectively

They are less busy with executing work and 'doing' the work of their teams. They have clarity on why and how to achieve goals.

Choose to inspire & unlock performance

They resist telling their people what to do or talking at them. They create ownership and commitment through enquiry.

Listen for what's important & what's at risk

They pick up on expressions, body language and other cues to initiate exploration and identify challenges.

Ask great questions & promote deeper thinking

Their presence and deep listening guide them to ask relevant, heart-of-the-issue questions to surface concerns and blockers.

Commit to honouring personal values — theirs & others'

They demonstrate a strong awareness of what knocks them off balance and makes them inconsistent. They do the same for others.

Support & empower people to solve & fix

They resist stepping in to fix or do-over someone else's work. They manage their boundaries and instead support their people to do their own heavy-lifting and create accountability.

Make decisions with evidence & confidence

They take steps to validate or overturn their own doubts and assumptions. Their confidence comes from securing reasonable certainty and truth.

Lead change & innovation

Being of a growth-mindset, they encourage and support improvement and innovation, making distinctions between what's working well and what could be much better.

Have comfort with accountability & difficult conversations

They have current knowledge of their people's strengths and ambitions. They are skilled at creating alignment, surfacing blockers, and contracting with compassion.

Advocate for influence & inclusivity

They operate with fairness and sensitivity. They know their own value and can articulate the values of others, and do so readily.

Intentionally experiment with questions & phrases

They are sensitive and mindful of their use of language and how their words are received in different contexts. They observe their impact and refine for next time.

The visibility of coach-leaders and the observable practice of Leaders Who Coach™ skills determine how much of a Coaching Culture an organisation has.

Coaching Cultures exist in organisations where the majority of leaders, at all levels and across all functions, demonstrate and model observable coach-leadership skills in one-to-one and team meetings, including under pressure. People processes reinforce coach-leader skills. Adoption is frictionless and rewarded.

For a coaching culture to be truly embedded and impactful to people and the bottom-line, there need to be Leaders Who Coach™ in all functions or departments at the senior-most levels. This ensures that skills are in daily practice and being modelled in one-to-one and team meetings, in negotiations during planning projects, building assets and serving customers, and even under pressure.

If you'd like to learn more about coach-leadership and coaching cultures, you'll find a wealth of resources here:

https://betterconversations.co/rulebook/#resources

And for course details, see the end of The Rulebook and visit us online here:

https://betterconversations.co/leaders-who-coach

Look out for the videos *The 7 Signatures of Coaching Cultures* and *The Challenges of Leadership & Why Leaders Who Coach™ Handle Them Better.*

You'll find even more examples of how coach-leaders apply their skills and more question and phrase suggestions to common people performance and productivity challenges, including delegating, difficult conversations, underperformance and contracting for accountability and wellbeing.

Your Invitation

♥

I invite the leader in you to...

Event: **Experience the power of coaching conversations**

Location: **In your one-to-one & team meetings**

Time/Date: **Minute-to-minute, every day**

Come as: **Your messy & imperfect self**

Theme: **Experimentation**

Treasure Hunt: **88 ✦ Questions & Phrases ✦**

Directions:
Follow your personal values
Watch for blind spots

Celebrate:
Becoming an inspiring & empowering leader

Companion Resources

I hope this Rulebook becomes your go-to for your entire career and life. In support of your exploration, you will find links to free companion resources at:

https://betterconversations.co/rulebook/#resources

Including...

YouTube Channel @BetterConversations

https://youtube.com/BetterConversations

For coach-leadership videos, shorts and playlists, including:

Stop creating risk when you delegate
Leadership Roadmap — 7 reasons to have one
Layoffs and healing conversations
Tolerating underperformance
How to ask for help at work & avoid overwhelm
Unstuck in 5 minutes with 5 coaching conversation questions
How to give advice to your direct reports
18 ways conversations go wrong
How leading with integrity affects your reputation
Effective listening on video conference calls
8 ways to run snappier, energising meetings
Why stepping up and letting go is hard

And more....

Better Conversations Podcast

On Apple, Audible, Google, Spotify & other fine places.

Blog+

https://betterconversations.co/blog/
For articles, posts & videos

88 Questions & Phrases PDF Download & Feedback Conversations Infographic

In the free Rulebook Mini-Course, you can download all 88 Questions & Phrases in this Rulebook, where you'll also find our Feedback Conversations Infographic (with video tutorials) for you to download covering:

Effective questions & phrases
Creative alignment to build generosity
Contract to secure commitment
Giving feedback remotely
Body language & non-verbal cues
Defensive & switching off signals

Mental health
Our brain & hormones in conversations
Conflict & strong misalignment
Team meetings & online group chats
Common mistakes to avoid

https://betterconversations.co/rulebook/#mini-course

Follow Better Conversations

YouTube: https://www.youtube.com/BetterConversations

LinkedIn: https://linkedin.com/company/BetterConversations/

Facebook: https://www.facebook.com/BetterConversations

Instagram: https://www.instagram.com/bettaconvos/

TikTok: https://www.tiktok.com/@betterconversations.co

Follow Sehaam Cyrene

LinkedIn: https://www.linkedin.com/in/sehaam/

Instagram: https://www.instagram.com/TawKwrd

The Rulebook Mini-Course

Leaders Who Coach™
Module 1 (Self-Paced):
Personal Values & Blind Spots

Raise your conversation game with our FREE Mini-Course (CPD Certified) and free community membership. You can enjoy bitesize exercises about your personal values and blind spots that impact your conversations in leadership, as explored by Sehaam in this Rulebook.

https://betterconversations.co/rulebook/#mini-course

★ RULE #1
EARN PERMISSION TO SPEAK

Quale /ˈkweɪli/
noun. a quality or property as perceived or
experienced by a person

HAVING A HISTORY TOGETHER
IS NOT ENOUGH

Having a history together or simply being in a meeting together does not guarantee sufficient levels of trust for the current conversation. Our conversation partner can still be resistant to our point of view. So how can we earn permission to speak?

If we think of trust as an important currency in our relationships, then the existence of trust can lead to good conversations. However, to have known each other a long time does not mean there are always sufficient levels of trust for the conversation we are currently in.

Unconsciously, we might experience the tension like this:

Wait a minute. Just because we are having a conversation... that does not guarantee I am open to listening to you. I may be present in front of you, but emotionally I may not have granted you permission to speak or share your opinion.

Also, when we think about breaking trust, we tend to think of the big and obvious ways it happens like lying, leaking confidential information, being unfair, or bullying. But trust can be broken during a conversation too — by not listening, being distracted, making assumptions before our conversation partner has spoken, discounting what they say, or simply not being interested in their point of view.

These mistakes make already difficult conversations even harder.

And so, as your conversation partner experiencing this breakdown in trust, I can hear you but I am withholding my full engagement or receptiveness to what you are saying. I do this because in this conversation — at this point in time — there is an insufficient level of trust from me towards you. And that's because you haven't made me feel good or validated me, or perhaps what you are saying is unclear and I have not felt listened to. Maybe I even feel disrespected and discounted.

As a result, I feel you are talking at me instead of being in conversation with me.

WHEN WE TALK _AT_ PEOPLE, WE TOUCH A NERVE

The vagus nerve to be exact, which is possibly the most important nerve in our body. It's a long meandering bundle of motor and sensory fibres that link the brainstem to the heart, lungs, gut and sex organs — affecting how we breathe, how our heart pumps blood and how we experience sex.

When we feel stressed, tired or anxious, or even hold a bad posture, our vagus nerve becomes inflamed. When we manage and process our emotions, there's an exchange of data between our vagus nerve and our heart, brain and gut, which is why we have a strong gut reaction to intense mental and emotional states.

It's the vagus nerve that's responsible for regulating our fight-or-flight stress response as well as our rest-and-digest or tend-and-befriend response. What's wonderful about the vagus nerve is that it's like a full body antenna, reading when situations are safe and when situations pose a threat to us, or irritate us. Like being talked at.

When you talk at me and I don't like what you are saying, my vagus nerve becomes inflamed. My body is flooded with cortisol (the stress hormone), I tense up and become less generous towards you. I become more judgemental and trust you less. I start to shut down, feel resistant to your ideas and unwilling to share my most important thoughts, ideas and worries with you.

When you're really in conversation with me, I get good readings from my vagus nerve. My system becomes flush with oxytocin (the connection hormone), I relax and *feel in sync with you. I might even let the conversation over-run. Emotional connection and creative thinking are easy because my trust towards you is strong. We're generating energy. Exchanging ideas and building on them is invigorating. Now I can trust you with my most important thoughts.*

So, if we're trying to influence someone or want them to take on board our counsel or advice, **talking at** someone is definitely not the way to go.

To influence or gain permission to speak, we first need to make the other person feel heard and understood; building up trust levels in the current conversation and earning their consent to share our opinion.

After some grounding and emotional connection work, this feels like the most natural thing to do for Leaders Who Coach™. Here are some things you can do to be in conversation with someone and gain their permission to speak.

DON'T GET PARANOID,
GET INTENTIONAL ✦

Don't get paranoid about how you're showing up in conversations. You're probably getting many of the basics right and you can build on that by becoming more intentional and practising these four conversation skills and habits.

Get clear about what you want to say, share or explore

The best negotiators prepare for every stage of the deal. You should prepare for every conversation, even if it's just 2 minutes beforehand to get in the zone, even if you don't know exactly what will be discussed.

Try reminding yourself of the last conversation, reflecting on any useful plans, names or interests the other person has. This gives a place to reconnect and quickly establishes a foothold of trust — who doesn't love it when other people remember something important to us?

If you do know what the conversation is going to be about, take more time to prepare — you might need 10 minutes or more. Get clear about what you know, the gaps in your knowledge or understanding (what you don't know), the key points of your position, the logic of your position, and what may be of interest/concern from their perspective.

Learn to be present and listen deeply

Distractions, people passing by or ducking in to say hello, apps pinging, phones buzzing, and eating during a conversation all reduce your ability to be present. Even if you reckon you're still listening, you've missed a lot and your conversation partner will feel it instantly (that vagus nerve never goes to sleep). The moment you're distracted could be the instant they choose to not share more important details.

Start by turning off things that will ping, close doors, talk somewhere quiet and try to have both of you sitting without the rest of the office in your view, or better still with your back to anyone who may pass by and think you're accessible. It goes without saying that for sensitive conversations you need a private and noise-sealed space. Despite appearances, many office rooms are not private at all and everyone can hear your conversation.

And like meditating, if your mind starts to wander to other thoughts, judgements, meetings or people, keep bringing it back to the person in front of you. Learn to notice when you have stopped listening and started your own internal monologue.

It takes practice to build up listening stamina but your conversation partner will notice and appreciate your focus and attention.

Ask good questions

Alongside deep or active listening, asking good questions is a top skill of Leaders Who Coach™. Asking good questions is not about asking a smart question or catching someone out on something they haven't considered. It's about helping your people grow and helping people think more deeply about their situation.

Ask permission to share your thoughts and perspectives

So you've prepared for the conversation, you've been present and listened deeply, and you've been asking good questions that have taken your conversation partner to places that they couldn't go on their own. Their vagus nerve is calm and they feel a strong emotional connection with you, they trust you in this conversation.

Now is the optimal time to share your side of the story, your perspective. And you do it with a fuller understanding of the other person and how they arrived at the position they find themselves in, helping you adjust your approach if needed. You can then ask,

"Would you like to hear my position / thoughts on this?"

You've improved the odds of them granting you a *"Yes"* and being fully engaged and receptive to what you've got to say because there's trust. You've validated them by listening to them and by helping them think to deeper levels, opening them up to new possibilities.

You've not assumed to know their position. You've not assumed that your relationship grants you the right to speak into this conversation. You've not assumed that they would be interested in your point of view.

You haven't talked at them. You've been *in* **conversation** *with* **them**.

✦ QUESTIONS & PHRASES ✦

"Why is that important?"

To understand their priorities and drivers.

"You've mentioned [...] a few times. What's significant about that?"

Repetition often indicates that [...] is important.

"What's brought you to that conclusion?"

To surface sources that have influenced their thinking.

"What have you thought about already?"

To discover what legwork they've already done.

★ RULE #2
TRUST UNDERPINS REPUTATION

"There was once a dream that was Rome. You could only whisper it. Anything more than a whisper and it would vanish... it was so fragile. And I fear that it will not survive the winter." — Marcus Aurelius, Gladiator

ALL THE LITTLE BREACHES

As leaders, we rely a great deal on the fragile currency of trust. Fragile because we break it so easily, often it's because of a blind spot — a behaviour or way of speaking that we're not aware of doing that could be derailing our relationships or reputation.

Being more aware of these breaches and the consequences can help us adjust our behaviour so we do them less often. We can raise our game further by using our personal values as a guide to show up more consistently. Our peers and our team will feel safer and more trusting when we show up consistently.

This is so important in coach-leadership that discovering personal values is the first exercise leaders do on Leaders Who Coach™.

And before you head down the futile road of denial that you don't breach trust, check yourself, because the research tells us we all do it.

Lies and deception

They are so pervasive. Firstly, we have a propensity to lie, apparently 1-2 times a day, usually harmless excuses or lies to protect someone's feelings or cover up our own insecurities. Secondly, we're gullible. We're not very good at detecting a lie, and sometimes we actually want to be lied to. And the top reasons we lie are to cover up a mistake, financial and personal gain, to avoid people, and to create a better impression of ourselves.

Hidden agendas and nasty surprises

We do this by deception or distraction, we dodge questions, gate-crash meetings just so we're seen, claim other people's hard work as our own, or charm someone into being a scapegoat for our mistakes.

False praise and compliments

We register a dislike in our own feelings and then we try to compensate by saying something opposite, sometimes to manipulate, sometimes to distract. But our words don't match our body language or facial expressions. We may think we've got away with it, but no, the other person has spotted it. People are just too polite to call you on it but they do walk away with a bad feeling about you.

Incompetence and absentee leadership

Incompetence is a major cause of distrust because, at a primal level, it puts our own survival at risk. Absentee leadership is when you show up to work but don't do very much. We certainly wouldn't trust a boss like this to support us or advocate for us.

Blaming, finger-pointing and shaming

When we do this, we're effectively stripping away someone's dignity. This can be overt and public, or it can happen in private.

Exclusion, intentional and unintentional

Intentional exclusion is the worst. We do it when we fear losing the opportunity to shine and claim the credit for something. Unintentional exclusion is an unconscious bias towards particular members of our team. This can play out as suppressing marginalised employees from being their authentic selves, shutting them out from opportunities (including meetings) or discriminatory comments.

Misrepresentation or falsely claiming someone else's work

It's surprising how often people tell me they worry their boss will not represent them fairly at a meeting with important stakeholders and decision-makers. Or equally unsettling, that their boss or a peer might take credit for the work of their team.

Disrespecting someone's time and effort

Trust is broken when we rock up late to a meeting, don't show up, or worse reschedule for what seems to be a less important event. And equally not thanking someone for their time and effort reduces their generosity towards us. It costs nothing to say *"Thank you."*

THE ANTIDOTE? INTEGRITY ✦

Choosing to lead with integrity affects our reputation. Our reputation can mean we get hired quickly and can help us secure investment in ourselves or our organisation. It's our reputation that draws great talent towards us, makes people want to be on our team and attracts entities that want to collaborate or partner with us. This is one of the reasons that Leaders Who Coach™ are ahead of their peers.

Leading with integrity is about honouring our own values consistently and, at the same time, noticing and responding to other people's values.

So, what does leading with integrity look like?

There's a lot in here but let me offer two things to think about:

1. Values are the principles, beliefs and attitudes that guide our decisions and our behaviours. We all have a unique collection of values. Which values you hold are personal to you. For example, you might hold Achievement, Balance, and Community to be really important to you, and someone you work with holds Determination, Greatness and Respect as values that drive their behaviour.

Honouring our own values consistently means honouring

them even when we're stressed or the decision isn't to our own advantage. We stay true to our values. For some of us, it isn't even a matter of choice. This consistency in how we respond to situations is what people experience of us when we're in conversation, negotiating, providing feedback, advocating for others, or dealing with a crisis.

2. It's not about giving up our values for someone else's. It's about inviting those of others in. Noticing other people's values is about having the flexibility or agility to respond in ways that say,

"I love that you enjoy that!"

"I get how that's important to you."

"Your [value] is front-and centre on this one."

For example, someone you're leading may have a very different set of values to you. That's very challenging for many of us because we use different language, sometimes more feeling language and sometimes more technical language. These alone create barriers — we can't get past the language sometimes. It also has a lot to do with things like first impressions, how we're wired and how we're interpreting other people's behaviours.

YOU GET ME ✦

To be a values-driven leader, you need to tune into your own values at any given moment and appreciate what value someone is speaking from. Remember, we don't have to adopt someone else's value — we just have to invite them into the conversation space, make an emotional connection or even a logic or reason-based connection. We all connect with the world in different ways.

Being able to express your values and someone else's values in a conversation in tangible ways that relate to the work that needs doing or a project plan can sound something like this,

"I know the quality of the work is important to you, so help me understand what we cannot compromise on and what aspects we can negotiate on."

In this example, 'quality' is a key value for them and 'collaboration' is a key value for you.

It's this ability to speak "two languages" that sets exceptional leaders apart from regular leaders. It's this experience of us, our ability to honour our values and to communicate it clearly, that people take away and remember.

So, leading with integrity is about honouring our values consistently AND "getting people", understanding other people's values. Then responding in ways that are intentional and sensitive.

This builds a good reputation. We'd all go the extra mile for someone who leads with integrity like this.

CONSISTENCY KEEPS TRUST ALIVE

Acting consistently shows up in what we do and how we say things. How we do things is unique to each of us, but it's the consistency that builds trust with others.

Your values drive your behaviour in predictable ways

When we reflect on our values, we're more likely to act in ways that honour them. They affect how we respond — whether we notice others' needs, what we act on and our hopes for others. Allowing our values to drive our behaviour makes it easy to show up consistently.

Speak truthfully with care for the listener

Actively finding ways to speak truthfully and taking care with our choice of words and timing mean that our message can land in the best possible way. We want to ensure that the other person doesn't shut down or feel threatened but gets a clear signal that we want to help.

Acknowledge the values of others, speak into them

Holding our own values does not come at the expense of denying the values of others. Instead, it helps us to notice a value that the other person may be acting on, offering up great opportunities to link a person's goals back to their values, especially when they're lacking in motivation or feeling a little lost.

Check yourself when under pressure

As a leader who coaches we need to understand our darker side, know our own triggers, and when we're likely to show up at less than our best. We need a way then to check ourselves that prompts us to stop, take a break, rebalance and then decide on the best course of action.

Own your mistakes and behaviours, be ready to apologise

We're not perfect and we will make mistakes. We are human. But even our errors present opportunities to act with integrity, by owning them and being ready to apologise. People who trust us are very willing to forgive us. Demonstrating an acceptance of our own vulnerability makes it okay for others to own their mistakes and moments of madness too.

Be ready to listen and appreciate feedback as gifts

It takes a lot of mental preparation and guts to give someone in a leadership role feedback. That's why many leaders don't hear it directly from their team but instead read it on a 360-performance report. If someone does give you feedback, it's likely that their own values compelled them to speak up, and that not to say something would mean compromising on who they hope they are. Their intention is to address the imbalance they feel and to make things better. This feedback offers us valuable data. That's what makes them gifts.

Discover your personal values and blind spots with our free Rulebook Mini-Course that accompanies this book.

Learn how to better prepare for and hold feedback

conversations with our Feedback Conversations Infographic (with video tutorials) which covers:

Effective questions & phrases
Creative alignment to build generosity
Contract to secure commitment
Giving feedback remotely
Body language & non-verbal cues
Defensive & switching off signals
Mental health
Our brain & hormones in conversations
Conflict & strong misalignment
Team meetings & online group chats
Common mistakes to avoid

https://betterconversations.co/rulebook/#mini-course

✦ QUESTIONS & PHRASES ✦

"Help me understand…"

Allows your direct report to explain how they see it
in their own words.

"Let me know if you think I've misunderstood anything."

Gives them permission to self-advocate.

"In what way have I contributed to this situation?"

Inviting honest feedback opens up accountability
in both directions.

"I'm sorry, that wasn't my intention."

A simple apology goes a very long way
towards repairing damage.

"How does the situation need to be different or better for you?"

Creates space for them to take their needs,
feelings and values seriously.

"I'm hearing that this [event or way of being] is very important to you."

Noticing someone's values can deepen their self-awareness.

"How can I best support you with that?"

Encourages them to ask for help because
asking for help is hard to do.

★ RULE #3
ZIP IT OR MISS IT

"Saying nothing sometimes says the most." — Emily Dickinson

THE POWER OF DEEP LISTENING

People talk about active listening. I prefer to call it deep listening because it encompasses what is said and what is not said — body language, posturing, micro-expressions and the whole richness of human expression that we haven't fully understood yet.

Why is it so important? And what does it look and feel like?

Our spoken words alone can never fully express what the 'everything' of an issue means to us. Add to that the dynamics of power, hierarchy, confidence, empathy, safety, trust, preparedness, and the complexity of the situation itself, and that what someone shares with us can be a sliver of what's really going on in their heads.

As leaders, we need to be able to pick up on as much of the 'everything' as possible AND manage our own responses effectively. And that requires two things.

First, it requires that we use all our faculties and tune into our observation antenna to pick up on what someone says AND what they don't say, as well as noticing how they say things, if they're striving to veil their real feelings and any shifts in their energy or posture. These cues are signposts to those 'everythings' that our direct report or conversation partner doesn't know how to express or feels uncomfortable voicing.

Second, it requires that we respond sensitively and appropriately to what we're picking up on, so we can support our conversation partner in their thinking. And that includes how we use language to share our observations and how we use questions to gain permission and explore those observations. As leaders, the responsibility of how we respond to what a person says is ours. In other words, we need to regulate our own emotions and respond in a helpful way.

Deep listening creates growth and self-awareness by offering up opportunities to surface potential risks and blockers to work getting done.

So, deep listening is important because listening invites growth. Growth between you and your direct report. It's here that we build understanding and strengthen our relationships — increasing trust, emotional connections, and raising oxytocin levels.

THE WHO ENERGY MODEL™

The Who Energy Model™ is designed for Leaders Who Coach™. It illuminates for us what our leadership role is really all about — helping our direct reports create shifts in their thinking to achieve new and better outcomes and reach their goals quicker.

'Who' a person is, at a given point in time, sits at the heart of the problem AND the solution. In other words, what a direct report wants to do and how they want to get there becomes clear once they have confidence in WHO they're being.

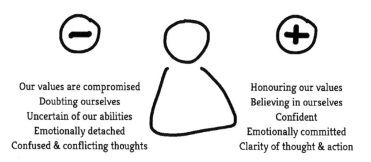

Our values are compromised	Honouring our values
Doubting ourselves	Believing in ourselves
Uncertain of our abilities	Confident
Emotionally detached	Emotionally committed
Confused & conflicting thoughts	Clarity of thought & action

Most of us are good at knowing what to do when we're in a Who-Positive state of mind and energy, and really struggle when we're feeling Who-Negative. As leaders, our role and priority is to empower others by encouraging and supporting a shift in their energy and perspective towards Who-Positive.

Once we've helped our direct report to find their Who-Positive and clarity of mind, then from there what we find is that defining the destination — the WHAT and HOW they want to get there — becomes apparent much more easily to them.

You can learn more about The Who Energy Model™ at

https://betterconversations.co/rulebook/#resources

PRACTISE DEEP LISTENING ✦

Slow down, be patient

Slowing down and being more patient means you can notice your direct report's energy and your brain has time to process your observations and catch-up with your other thoughts. Curb your desire to jump in with your ideas and solutions because this limits the other person's enthusiasm to think or contribute to the conversation – if you handle it right, there'll be plenty of time for you to share your thoughts later on.

Don't expect people to be able to articulate their thoughts perfectly the first time they share them. Let people have two or three goes at expressing themselves. Summarise and check you've heard them right, then let them speak some more. That has the effect of externalising the situation they are talking about, taking it out of their own heads, and it allows them to see things from the outside. This can create amazing clarity and gives them a chance to re-evaluate things.

Leave longer silences

Recognising that some thoughts take courage to express, it's good to leave longer silences in conversations as invitations to say more. We do an enormous amount of self-censoring. We prefer to hold back to be on the safe side rather than risk expressing an opinion we think might get knocked down or offend.

So, leaving longer silences after someone speaks invites them to keep talking. Make sure you acknowledge that courage by saying something like,

"I appreciate you sharing that with me, thank you."

And take care how you use that information — they've just taken a leap and shared something that's important to them – don't break that trust.

All-in all, when someone is talking with us, we're lucky if we absorb 25% of what they're expressing both verbally and non-verbally — and probably a lot less than that for our online exchanges. As leaders, we need to absorb an extra 30-50% if we're going to pick up on the cues that help us explore more, ask good questions, and grow our people.

And when you absorb more information through deep listening, your conversations will feel different. You should feel calmer, more aware, and your direct report should feel that you get them. Talking with you is clarifying and deeply satisfying.

Watch your own discounting behaviour

Discounting behaviour can either be words or actions that devalue what the other person is saying or feeling.

It sounds like, *"You're wrong"*, *"That's rubbish"*, *"I don't believe that's true"* or *"Really?"* delivered with a disbelieving or even condescending tone.

Discounting behaviour looks like checking your phone, having a quick exchange with another colleague, or even shortening the meeting for something else that's 'come up'.

Our discounting behaviour diminishes our own presence in a conversation and therefore our ability to listen deeply. And we create a distraction — we break their flow of thought. We're saying, *"You're not that important to me"* and they lose trust in us. If there are other people involved, they're picking up this signal too and, in this way, we disempower the person talking.

EXTRA CONSIDERATIONS
ON VIDEO CALLS

Video or online calls can be tricky because staring at a screen full of faces, poor network connection and interruptions from deliveries do not equal the most natural way of engaging with other people. So how can you make it easier to listen effectively?

Beyond choosing a quiet space, being on time and making sure you're prepared, there are several other ways you can stay engaged...

Demonstrate you're listening by not interrupting the speaker. Too many *"mmms"* and *"yeahs"* have the potential to knock out the audio and cause that awkward *"Did you want to say something?"* Instead, nod your head, give people a thumbs up to show your agreement, or raise your hand to ask a question or to contribute your thoughts.

Limit your interactions on other channels, like chat, because even if you think they can't see your hands, the rest of your body and your gaze are totally giving you away!

Another way we can show we're listening is by **changing our physical position**. Look into the camera or at the person speaking — ideally, your camera is positioned close to the video of the person you're in conversation with so you can do both at the same time. Shift your physical position in relation to what they're saying. You can lean forward or put your hand to your chin. These are visual cues that tell the person speaking that we're listening deeply and we're interested.

How we respond verbally is an indicator of how effectively we're listening. We don't have to respond every time, but what we say or what questions we ask reveal a lot about how well we're listening.

Don't multitask by working on other unrelated documents or, for someone working from home, doing household chores. It doesn't just give us all a headache and create a distraction away from someone speaking, it's just plain rude.

If you're chairing the meeting, you need to **be the guardian of this meeting space**. Making sure the call is conducive to good listening, that you model effective listening, and actively invite people who are showing high levels of interest to contribute. And it's absolutely your job as a leader to gently remind people to minimise their distractions on the call, out of respect for everyone and to ensure the quality of the meeting time.

✦ QUESTIONS & PHRASES ✦

"How is it affecting you / your team?"
To explore impact and consequences on key stakeholders.

"How did that play out?"
Reflection helps to evaluate what worked well
and what could be better.

"Your energy picked up / dropped off there... "
To expand self-awareness of themselves.

"I'm sensing... / I'm noticing..."
Naming something unspoken also expands self-awareness.

"What does [...] mean to you?"
Avoids projecting our meaning onto them
and invites elaboration.

"What makes you think that?"
To understand how they reached that conclusion.

"How does that influence how you see things?"

To explore the impact of any filters or bias they're applying.

★ RULE #4
SIMPLE QUESTIONS

"I cannot teach anybody anything. I can only teach them to think." — Socrates

QUESTIONS ARE BEAUTIFUL

Questions are the most under-used technique in leadership for gaining buy-in, creating emotional connection and in problem solving.

I've seen questioning used to undermine confidence, interrogate in a manner that scapegoats, and sabotage team cohesion. Leaders who use questions in this way are in fact self-sabotaging and breaking down team culture. Which is a shame because, when used well, questioning can be a deeply rewarding approach to growing people, managing risks and building loyalty.

When we help our direct reports to think more deeply about a situation they're facing, the result is that we enable them to come up with their own solutions. And those are the best ones because those are the ones they are most deeply emotionally connected to – their solutions, not ours – and are most likely to follow-through on.

So, as long as they are good solutions, you're onto a winner.

TO EXPAND THINKING
AND CURIOSITY ✦

Use questions to expand thinking and curiosity. The ancient philosopher Socrates believed that questioning is intimately connected with critical thinking. So, borrowing his approach as psychotherapists of today have, we can guide our people through a set of questions to expand their thinking and curiosity, all the way through to resolving their own situation. Sort of like a mind map but in a conversation.

✦ QUESTIONS & PHRASES ✦

"Do you have an outcome in mind?"

Invites your direct report to articulate their objectives.

"What might be another interpretation of what happened?"

Invites them to consider alternative narratives.

"Where is the disconnect?"

Surfaces when and where misunderstandings may have happened.

"I wonder what was missed?"

Depersonalises errors and invites exploration.

"What's the worst that could happen?"

Talking about the scary space makes it less scary
and generates agency.

"What value does that provide?"

Creates clarity for decision-making.

TO CREATE FORWARD MOMENTUM ✦

Use questions to create forward momentum. By that I mean, help your direct report to explore their situation in a way that moves them forward and gets them unstuck. From feeling defeated and out of control towards feeling energised and positive. Exploring options and consequences is one example of creating forward momentum, because trying things on for size helps us evaluate whether to rule out an option or to act on it.

✦ QUESTIONS & PHRASES ✦

"What could be holding you back?"

Naming things is the start of exploring them.

"What do you think your options are?"

Speaking out their current analysis makes their real preferences clearer.

"Which of those would be good to explore further?"

Ensures we're focused on what's most important to them.

"What needs to happen?"

Focuses them on their essential next step, which may not be what they prefer to do.

"How can you test those ideas and assumptions?"

To create confidence in their final decision.

TO GROW PEOPLE ✦

Leaders Who Coach™ experiment with and test out different questions until they find the phrasing and delivery that feels most natural to them. This approach builds their confidence and mastery when they're in growth conversations with their direct reports.

How many of your questions in conversations with your direct reports are truly intentional? As in you ask them questions with the primary goal of growing the person in front of you, and not just to gather information (like status updates).

Most of the time we dominate conversations with our opinions, we talk at our people, or we plainly tell them what to do. That approach leaves little room for growth for anyone, you or your direct report.

Granted, sometimes under pressure, the most pragmatic approach is to give direction or instruct someone. But the bigger game is in growing your people whenever the opportunity comes up, which is the rest of the time. This is how you grow and prepare them for those pressured or crisis moments.

Get to the detail

Questions help draw out the knot of details and feelings that our direct report has in relation to a problem. Asking questions that untie this knot is important because there's a high probability that the solution is sitting right in that knot — in the details and their feelings, and their attachment to a specific outcome.

You could try asking,

"What's coming up for you as you say that?"

in a non-judgmental way to invite self-reflection of those deeper feelings.

Gain clarity

Then there are questions that probe more deeply and encourage us to elaborate as a way of gaining clarity. For most of us, what we first say or articulate isn't necessarily coherent or joined up thinking. That's normal. So, a series of questions that get us to elaborate are the best way to sort through the mess in our heads and the feelings in our hearts.

Try asking,

"How is that significant?"

to invite exploration and separation of the threads of thoughts, facts and feelings, and possibly how they relate to their personal values.

Less than 10% of leaders are good at conversations with their direct reports. It just takes practice in the way of Leaders Who Coach™.

Highlight assumptions

And then how about challenging their assumptions and limiting beliefs? This is an advanced conversation approach of Leaders Who Coach™ because it requires a level of comfort to both challenge someone's thinking and be compassionate in the same breath. To not be triggered by what we're hearing and get hijacked by our own thoughts, but instead continue listening deeply and holding the space for the other person.

If your direct report or conversation partner trusts you and knows that you always hold a safe space for them to talk, then it's game on.

Guess what's sitting in there? Yep, all the things that are going to stop them from following through on something including risks, insecurities, and misunderstandings. Let's get all those on the table so they can be clear that they know what they need to be sure about.

Still with me? So, what gaps do they need to fill, and what information is missing that they need to make the right call.

Try asking,

"Why does this decision need to be made now?"

great for challenging an assumption. Or,

"How true is that?"

said with much compassion, this can help challenge a limiting belief.

Uncover the truth

As a leader who is helping your direct report to think a situation through and get clarity, you can help them work out what questions they should be asking and what questions they need to go away and find answers to. Proper answers, not more opinions and bad interpretations. So, what questions do they need to ask to find evidence and hard facts.

Try asking,

"How can you confirm that?"

because it affords them an opportunity to either gain certainty about their decision, or to become open to an alternative.

All this creative and safe thinking is generating a new awareness of themselves and within themselves, of how they are viewing the situation.

Explore new options

And then once our direct report can see their situation clearly, and their trust in us is high, we can invite them to consider alternative explanations or possibilities, and the consequences of those alternatives alongside their initial ideas.

So try asking,

"What are you prepared to try?"

to get that exploration going and then

"How far can you take that idea?"

so that they can begin to get familiar and comfortable with the possible outcomes.

And guess what? We've helped move the conversation forward.

Also remember, that if our conversation partner doesn't trust us or we don't have a deep emotional connection, we can't do this. We haven't earned their permission to go deep inside their head and their hearts.

This is a very privileged position to be in because wonderful stuff happens here. Our direct report can now begin to imagine or design a different outcome, by taking the best steps when they can see things clearly.

There's no shortcut to getting all of this right. Sometimes words will fall out wrong. No big deal. Have another go at asking the question. It shows humility and good intention, and your direct report will appreciate you even more for it.

Support yourself in growing people by learning to notice their personal more easily. The secret is to start by noticing your own values with our free Rulebook Mini-Course accompanying this book:

https://betterconversations.co/rulebook/#mini-course

IT'S A QUESTION OF HYGIENE ✦

As well as being spontaneous in conversations and directly responding to what your direct report is saying and thinking, it's important that you **keep your questions succinct**. Succinct questions are easier for people to process – they don't have to decipher what we mean and it doesn't interrupt their flow of thought.

For the same reasons, we need to **avoid stacking our questions**, which is asking more than one question in each exchange. If we ask 2-3 questions in one breath, we put people in the predicament of trying to work out which question to answer first, cluttering up their thinking and their response. This is particularly challenging to those of us who are neurodivergent and appreciate logical or uncluttered thinking and questioning.

Let go of using leading or loaded language that generates feelings of high emotional charge. These types of questions and phrases are intended to sway our opinion or persuade us towards a certain point of view or outcome.

For example, instead of *"Do you think it's because you always over-react?"*, we can ask

"What do you believe contributes to that happening?"

Or instead of *"Could it be that you don't like him as much as your old boss and that's what's causing the tension between you?"*, we can simply ask

"What differences are you seeing?"

Leading and loaded language derail the conversation and our relationships because they diminish trust in us and possibly irritate your direct report towards an opposing point of view as their counter-manoeuvre.

You want to ask open questions that generally begin with What, Why, When, Where, How and Who to invite elaboration.

Asking closed or dead-end questions, like *"Did you tell them?"* will typically give us a Yes or No answer, which stifles conversations. But if instead we ask,

"How did you tell them?"

we'll get a far richer response.

Take care with your tone when asking 'why' questions, as they can feel judgemental.

Which brings me to my next point. How we ask questions and when we ask them are also important – these are linked to the mood of the moment and what feels right to explore – so be thoughtful and intentional in your **tone and timing.**

And if all that doesn't motivate you to brush up on your questioning skills, then how about this. Some research tells us that **asking good questions can make people like us more**, which is likely to do with how asking good questions and giving our undivided attention makes people feel about themselves, releasing happy hormones in the process.

They like us and trust us more because we take a genuine interest in them. And that's what deepens their emotional connection to us as leaders.

★ RULE #5
OVERSHARING IS RISKY

"Vulnerability without boundaries is not vulnerability." — Brené Brown

"CAN YOU BE TOO VULNERABLE?"

This is a question that points to 'vulnerability without boundaries' that I get a lot from leaders who might be guilty of oversharing. The answer might be "Yes" but it depends on what is meant here by being 'too vulnerable'. And could being too vulnerable actually be creating more damage, more risk?

That's what I want to come back to, but first let's establish the context here.

Being vulnerable can happen when you're in conversation with someone and together you're talking about the really tough stuff, things that are going wrong, where emotions in the team may be running high, and there's a lot at stake. Where trust is fragile, or the decisions to be made are going to change your business massively, perhaps irreversibly... those tough conversations have the 3 key ingredients for being vulnerable as Brené Brown has defined for us: uncertainty, risk and emotional exposure.

THEY'RE WATCHING YOU,
ALL THE TIME

As a leader, you are a role model and everyone in your team and company is watching you all the time, because while what you say is important, how you say things and what you do provides far more accurate instruction.

In other words, your actions are more revealing than your words. For example, you may say creativity and innovation is important, but your behaviour actually reveals that you want people to do things your way, because that's what you reward, that's what gets publicly acknowledged, or that's what gets funding.

Brené Brown talks about the benefits to your culture if you, as a leader, can move towards showing vulnerability – for example, *"I don't have all the answers", "I need your help to get there", "I made a mistake".* It sets the example and the conditions for being creative and encouraging innovation. It's what I call experimentation. If you have a culture that embraces experimentation, then you'll probably see lots of evidence of creativity and innovation.

SCARY IF YOU ARE UNCLEAR

But that's not easy to do if you don't have the skills to navigate those tough conversations, if you don't know what you stand for, if you don't know your own values and have little awareness of your blind spots (the things you overlook or do that are actually getting in the way).

It's also really tough to do if you don't have the conversation skills to understand what's going on in an exchange, why people are reacting or responding in a certain way, how you might be shutting people down, how you could express yourself in a way that keeps people listening to you, how you can create trust and safety, or how to invite people to speak more freely and think creatively.

Brené Brown talks about having courage and having comfort with feeling uncomfortable. But these things aren't easy to do and that's why being vulnerable feels scary...

...unless you're grounded, connected and great at conversations.

I would add 3 leadership capabilities that I teach Leaders Who Coach™ as essential to being vulnerable:

1.   You need to be grounded with a strong self-awareness

2.   You need to know how to connect emotionally with people

3.   You need great conversation skills

Having courage is much easier when you have these 3 things.

Back to the question, *"Can you be too vulnerable?"*

In all the talk about vulnerability and leadership, we tend to overlook the point at which oversharing is unhelpful — and this is what I want to explore here.

When Brené Brown says, *"Vulnerability without boundaries is not vulnerability,"* she's asking us to think about why we're sharing and whether it's productive and appropriate.

This question, *"Can you be too vulnerable?"* is a constant conundrum for leaders. What they're really asking is *"How much is okay to share?"* and *"How much of my worries and issues is okay to share with my team, my direct reports, my peers or my boss even?"*

They are worried about oversharing because they're not clear on what is valuable and useful to share, as distinct from just offloading because they feel alone and want some relief or sympathy.

It's a tough place to be. And they are right to be worried because they could be introducing risk that need not be there.

You can become less fearful and more aware of what you stand for and of your own blind spots with our free Mini-Course:

https://betterconversations.co/rulebook/#mini-course

THE THINGS LEADERS
WORRY ABOUT

Leaders are making difficult decisions all the time. They're often feeling conflicted between being a good leader who is liked and making the right business call. They're looking over the cliff-edge.

Can I pay everyone this month? Are we going to close enough deals to survive this quarter?

If Amanda doesn't get a promotion this round, will she leave?

Zach is a technical genius but he's killing our culture.

James is my friend but he's underperforming and costing the business a lot of money.

Rather than securing funding, I'm being asked to make half my team redundant.

There's evidence that our supplier may be stealing our IP.

Thirty percent of our customers are threatening to end their subscriptions and I don't know how we're going to replace that revenue.

These are real worries that keep us awake at night. And often, there are no clean and simple answers. We start doubting ourselves and our judgments, and that causes us stress and anxiety.

So, as a leader who wants to be vulnerable, open and transparent, who wants to be a good leader...

WHAT'S OKAY TO SHARE?

Only you can come to the right choice for your situation — what's appropriate and productive. But when you are considering how much to share — all of it, some of it or none of it — ask yourself this:

Which option introduces the most *unacceptable* risk? That is, risk that will damage your culture or your business in ways you cannot reverse or undo.

Sharing too much might breach trust agreements or it might distract people from doing their best work or harm your culture. That could prove to be a wholly unacceptable risk, because collaboration becomes impossible, or delivery timelines and contracts are compromised.

Sharing too little or trying to put an unrealistic or positive spin on things, might also introduce doubt and distrust. Remember, people are watching your actions more than listening to your words. If there are problems, it's highly likely people already know about it, so denying or falling silent about them is interpreted as a deception. People reach their own conclusions and view you as less competent. Is that an unacceptable risk?

WHAT TO SHARE AND HOW

As a leader, you've got two considerations: one is figuring out what you're going to share, and the second is how that sharing will look.

The what

In figuring out what to share, it's helpful to talk it through with someone you trust and who is most likely to be impartial. It might be best that they are people outside your organisation, who can help you reach different perspectives, and who want to see you thrive. A mentor or leadership coach with substantial business experience is ideal.

Get clear on what you think, work through your conflicting thoughts and stress-test your options. You want to feel safe voicing difficult thoughts in a confidential thinking space, to explore and plan your approach, to be completely vulnerable and know there won't be a backlash. You want to prevent introducing risk into your business while you're still figuring things out.

The how

When it comes to the second point about how your sharing will look and feel, consider these questions:

1. How can you use it to focus your people?
2. What can you be personally vulnerable about?
3. How will you share the information and the ask with each affected group?

In other words, what discomfort are you experiencing that is useful to share and that will not introduce a risk that is unacceptable? And how do you want each group to receive that information?

Sharing may still involve uncertainty, risk and emotional exposure, but what you choose to share won't cross a boundary of being inappropriate or unproductive.

TIME TO BE INTENTIONAL AND STRATEGIC

Leaders Who Coach™ learn to be both intentional and strategic in how they approach their conversations and what they choose to share. They factor in all their stakeholders, from individuals to teams or groups. And don't forget, there may also be contractual and legal aspects in these conversations.

If you are grounded as a leader with a strong self-awareness (like knowing your values and your blind spots), and **you're emotionally connected** to your people, working out your approach is much easier. The added bonus is that the focus is less on your courage and more on the impact that sharing certain information has on others and the business.

If you've got great conversation skills, then you're even more capable of navigating those difficult knots by listening, asking useful questions, and responding in helpful ways that move the conversation forward. You can focus on the useful aspects of a situation that help people make good decisions, while making sure you're not inadvertently shutting conversations down.

So, being vulnerable and courageous is much easier when you've got these 3 capabilities: you're grounded, you're emotionally connected to people, and you have great conversation skills like Leaders Who Coach™.

These capabilities help you read your situation more accurately and respond appropriately. They help you work out how to be vulnerable in useful ways, instead of oversharing and overwhelming the people you rely on.

★ RULE #6
LESS HASTE, MORE STRATEGY

"The single biggest problem in communication is the illusion that it has taken place." — George Bernard Shaw

WE EXPECT TOO MUCH FROM ONE CONVERSATION

Breaking down one big, tricky conversation into phases, can relieve the pressure to agree or fix something in one single scheduled conversation.

It's a little unfair to expect so much from a single conversation. And yet we suffer such disappointment when we don't make the headway we had hoped. And it's unfair for our conversation partner too. We've probably been mulling an idea over for a long while, but we're betting everything on them being our cheerleader in less than an hour!

It's far less anxiety-loading to break down a conversation into a sequence of key phases: the socialising phase, the creative alignment phase, and the contracting phase. Complex, strategic or politically charged situations may need more time and multiple loops within each phase.

THE SOCIALISING PHASE

The socialising phase is a relatively low risk stage that's great for gauging the strength of people's opinions or reactions to your ideas. What might you be stepping into? Who is attached to the status quo or the outcome, and why?

It's good to know how deep the water is, where the swells are and how strong the undercurrents are!

You might have a few of these socialising conversations with lots of different stakeholders and decision-makers to map out the landscape.

Socialising conversations are characterised as being presented to individuals and groups with the lightness of a feather so as to be exploratory and non-threatening, with low emotional attachment so we can invite honest responses and be receptive to alternative or counter positions, and with an invitation to talk again further and more deeply in the future.

This approach and stance will help you work out what your next move needs to be.

THE CREATIVE ALIGNMENT PHASE

The creative alignment phase takes you to the next level of definition. What are people's positions and why? What concerns do they have? Where are the risks? What could go wrong? What could go great? What's the best approach? Why would those affected by it support it?

The socialising phase informs you about who these creative alignment conversations need to happen with. So you might talk to a smaller group of people or just one person. Again, you might find you need to have a few rounds of creative alignment conversations.

Permission to play a different role in conversations

Creative alignment is about uncovering the feelings, reservations and motivations people have about the situation, including the approach, impact, facts, evidence and data. You want to know about anything that could cause your initiative to fail. Equally, anything that could help speed up things is precious and valuable to know.

A large part of your role in creative alignment conversations — and possibly the most effective and influential — is to ask questions that help people think more deeply about the topic. How you do this is important.

If people feel judged and under pressure to say something smart or to come up with solutions straight away, they can't be creative and generous. There's too much cortisol and adrenaline (stress hormones) in their system.

Two important things to mention here — and Leaders Who

Coach™ will recall their own learning curve in appreciating these:

1. **You don't need to have all the answers** and sometimes it's easier to be detached and less triggered by what people say because you don't have the answers.

2. **Don't jump into 'solutioning' yet.** Whatever you come up with at this stage is not likely to be innovative or collaborative but heavily biased towards the regular way of doing things. This may draw lower levels of commitment or ownership from others.

There you go. I've just given you permission to <u>not</u> have an opinion and <u>not</u> have a solution. (And breathe.) You're welcome.

You can't hurry trust, you just have to wait

You can't rush this exchange of ideas and positions because it relies on building trust between you and your conversation partners. They may want to see what you do with the initial information they share with you before they give you any more.

Another reason we shouldn't rush the creative alignment phase of conversations is that time to reflect is a really important part of the thinking and evaluating process. Our brains need that time to make connections and come to a new level of awareness. Some realisations are only possible when we're doing something else, which allows our position to soften towards alternative opportunities. Familiarity and attachment to new ideas increases the longer we have time to sit with them.

It means that when we next come together to continue the conversation, we can be more nuanced and considered. Possibly even more open to other people's ideas that, at first, we rejected.

If you're thinking, *"But that's so slow. I just want to get in there and get stuff done,"* then this might help... Think of it as an approach that encourages generosity and emotional connection in your conversations. The more generous people feel, the more likely they are to share their best ideas with you. And the stronger the emotional connection between you, the quicker you'll be able to work through the harder parts of negotiating and contracting.

So, it's slower to begin with but it gets quicker and stronger later.

The Creative Alignment Phase in Feedback Conversations

Everything I've mentioned about the creative alignment phase is wholly relevant and critical to productive feedback conversations. Creative alignment builds generosity between us to open up, share mistakes, and collaborate towards something better and stronger.

For this type of conversation, you'll find question and phrase suggestions in the Feedback Conversations Infographic available as part of the resources and downloads in our free Rulebook Mini-Course accompanying this book. As well as video tutorials on common mistakes to avoid, the infographic gives you guidance on our brain and hormones, body language and non-verbal cues, defensive and switching off signals, and safe guarding mental health.

Enjoy the people you're in conversation with

Give yourself permission to enjoy just being in conversation with others, learning how they think and finding out what's important to them. This is just as important an aspect of leadership as strategising and getting stuff done. And it will show up in your manner, the way you make people feel and how loyal they feel towards you.

Furthermore, it's critical to the next phase.

THE CONTRACTING PHASE

The contracting phase is where we come to an agreement with all parties to the conversation and decision-making. It's where we negotiate and trade, make requests of each other and offer assurances. Divide up the work and responsibilities, agree the resources and the people we need to do the work. Discuss the consequences of good outcomes and bad ones, define the key explanations of why. And consider options and alternatives should we need to course-correct or react to an unexpected turn of events.

These contracting conversations are calorie-burning conversations so get a good night's sleep and have a sustaining meal beforehand to fuel your brain.

If you've built up trust and powerful levels of emotional connection with people, then contracting will be a truly enjoyable phase — you'll feel energised and hopeful. If you haven't, then this phase will be stressful, conflict-ridden, and physically and emotionally draining — if you get to this phase at all.

The Contracting Phase in Feedback Conversations

As with the creative alignment phase, the contracting phase is equally critical and often rushed through in feedback conversations. It is good contracting that increases ownership and follow-through success rates, making follow-up, accountability and course-correcting conversations easier.

Leaders think they do this well but then struggle with or avoid underperformance conversations.

You'll find guidance on contracting to secure commitment, resolve conflict and address strong misalignment, and giving feedback remotely, as well as mistakes to avoid, in the Feedback Conversations Infographic available in resources and downloads in our free Rulebook Mini-Course accompanying this book:

https://betterconversations.co/rulebook/#mini-course

✦ QUESTIONS & PHRASES ✦

A first invitation in the Socialising Phase to open up conversation:

"What are your thoughts on...?"

"What experience have you had with...?"

"Can I run something by you?"

To map out the current landscape and surface potential blockers and new opportunities in the Creative Alignment Phase:

"What's your position on this?"

"What concerns do you have?"

"What risks do you see?"

"What opportunities does this offer us?"

And then in the Contracting Phase:

"Where would be a good place to start?"
Giving others a voice invites co-ownership.

"Who do you need to speak to and find out...?"
To confer with other stakeholders affected by this opportunity.

"What could go wrong?"
To identify risks so you can eliminate or plan for them.

"What have we not thought of?"
Surfaces new ways or possible additional areas of resistance.

"What would make this even better?"
To make the idea even more compelling.

"What do you need from me so you can do ...?"
To find out what the other person needs in order to give you their support.

OH AND CONVERSATION PHASES
ARE NOT LINEAR

Leaders Who Coach™ know that conversations go forwards, backwards, and sideways. They can take turns no-one expected. Some stages need repeating. They can stall and they can breakdown. Conversations can take hours, days, weeks or even months — certainly the more complex or tricky topics will take longer.

As well as giving you more influence with people, stronger emotional connections will help things go smoother and move quicker because of the common ground you share.

Having a strategy for your conversations, understanding that people need to go through emotional states and thinking stages, and seeing your role as an enabler of the process, will go a long way towards reducing your frustration and anxiety towards others. You'll increase your success in those big, tricky conversations.

★ RULE #7

PUT SECOND IMPRESSIONS FIRST

"Our love of being right is best understood as our fear of being wrong." — Kathryn Schulz

WRONG. IN THE BLINK OF AN EYE

We judge people too quickly. The trouble is, first impressions aren't always accurate, and yet how we behave is heavily influenced by that first judgement. And in the end, nobody wins. So, what are we judging and how can we limit the risk to our relationships?

Are you ignorant, an idiot or just plain evil?

American journalist and author Kathryn Schulz wrote a book called *"Being Wrong — Adventures in the Margin of Error"*, with an in-depth analysis on human behaviour. In talking about our minds and our beliefs, she explains a common sequence that we go through when someone disagrees with us. It looks something like this.

> *When someone first disagrees with us, we*
> *conclude that it's just because they don't have the*
> *right information, they're ill-informed:*

"You're just ignorant."

When they still don't agree with us, we shake our heads, throw our hands in the air and accept that they just don't know how to use their brain properly:

"Idiot."

And finally, when they persist in disagreeing with us, they must be wilfully winding us up:

"You are pure evil."

It's easy to fall into these classic judgments, especially when we are fixated on our own pre-determined ideal outcome.

We judge others in less than a blink of an eye. 100-milliseconds to be precise. And that can have serious consequences on our own behaviour.

In some modest experiments by Janine Willis and Alexander Todorov conducted around 2005/2006 at Princeton University, they concluded that in as little as a tenth of a second of looking at someone, we judge them by their facial features of expression, known as physiognomy.

THE 5 TRAITS WE JUDGE
EACH OTHER ON

Without placing any time constraints on the participants in these experiments, they asked them to look at 70 photographs of amateur actors, 35 females and 35 males between the ages of 20 and 30. They 'neutralised' the images as much as possible so all the photos showed people in grey T-shirts and no distinguishing facial features — so the beardies, moustachioed were out and no-one wearing spectacles, earrings or make-up.

They asked the participants to judge on a 9-point scale (from 1 not at all, to 9 extremely) the degree to which the person in each picture met a certain trait. To cut a long study report short, they narrowed down the main traits as being **attractiveness, likability, trustworthiness, competence**, and **aggressiveness**.

So that's how we judge people. *"Do I like you? Can I trust you?"*

All from looking at their face in less than a blink of an eye. Everything is neat and sweet if you decide you like them. But let's be honest, how many times out of all the people you've met so far has that happened?

Of the 5 traits, attractiveness, likability, trustworthiness and competence relate to the opportunity for building emotional connections — making us feel generous due to increased levels of oxytocin and other feel-good hormones in our system.

Aggressiveness marks the introduction of stress and tension between us, as a result of increased cortisol and adrenaline.

We might be judging people at the point of being introduced

to them or just by clocking them in our view or in our peripheral vision.

THE RBF BIAS

We don't even have to be in conversation with someone to judge them. Oh no. Consider this — that person may be deep in focus or relaxed and resting. And I don't know about you, but I have the best RBF (resting b**** face) money can buy. Friends have said to me, *"You should smile more, you look lovely when you smile."* I appreciate now they were trying to tell me something.

But seriously, it's studied by psychologists, has its own meme and there's an entry on Wikipedia for it too! Resting A***hole Face (RAF) is the male version, apparently.

Basically, it's when we unintentionally hold a facial expression that reads *"I'm angry / annoyed / irritated / contemptuous"* when actually we're just chilling or deep in thought. Maybe it's a survival thing Mother Nature put in place because we're more vulnerable to physical attack when we're deep in thought and less aware of our surroundings, so our faces signal, *"Approach at your own risk."* I'll buy that made-up theory!

THE OXYTOCIN VS CORTISOL BATTLE

When we judge people too quickly, we're actually putting up emotional barriers to connecting with them, making us less likely to walk up to them and say hello. So, our oxytocin (connection hormone) levels are low and our cortisol (stress) levels are likely to be high. That now takes us a lot more intentional effort to overcome and find a way to connect with that person.

In this context, we go on to make incomplete, and often inaccurate interpretations of that person and their motives or intentions. This introduces risk into the 'relationship' and means we derail ourselves as leaders, creating reasons not to connect any more than is necessary.

Which means we won't reach out to them to just get to know them, we won't think to speak to them first before making decisions that affect them, giving them feedback will be harder, and we won't consider any influence they may have on our peers. Not enough oxytocin. Not enough generosity. And they'll pick up on our reluctance to get to know them because like us, their vagus nerve is taking situation readings as fast as ours is.

And when it comes to a disagreement, a misalignment or a conflict, there won't be enough emotional credit or willingness to find common ground and to work harder to resolve issues. So, with a bird's eye view, our judging too quickly means no-one comes out a winner.

Cortisol wins.

In the free Rulebook Mini-Course accompanying this book, you can learn more about how emotional connection and oxytocin can help unlock generosity in conversations with our Feedback Conversations Infographic PDF download and supporting video tutorials.

https://betterconversations.co/rulebook/#mini-course

SLOW DOWN, ESPECIALLY WHEN YOU DISAGREE

Leaders Who Coach™ learn that the trick to not judging too quickly is to slow down and ask questions because when we slow down, we buy ourselves time to re-evaluate our first impressions.

And when we disagree with someone, asking questions are a great way to avoid an amygdala hijack, stay in the conversation, and give our brains a practical and cognitive task. This approach is soothing to us. So long as we can listen deeply to what they are saying, we create the opportunity of getting to know them better and, over time, building an emotional connection.

And remember, if we still disagree, we don't have to express it in the moment. We could learn quite a bit more if we let go of that need to pronounce our disagreement. In a heated exchange, if you must say something, then barter — either ask for more time to think about their position or ask them to send you some alternative information to help you understand their position better.

And watch your body language too. We leak so many tells when we disagree.

By the way, what's your RBF or RAF?

✦ QUESTIONS & PHRASES ✦

"Hello, we haven't properly met yet.
Can we grab a coffee?"

No matter how much time has passed, we can make the first invitation.

"Tell me more…"

To buy ourselves time to listen for longer before responding.

"What does […] mean to you?"

To overcome assumptions and possible misunderstandings.

"I understand this about […], is that
your understanding?"

To surface areas of misalignment that are leading to conflict.

"What have your inputs been so far?"

To understand how their thinking has been informed.

"What might the consequences of that be?"

To identify potential pitfalls together.

"I need time to consider this fully.
Let's reconvene next week."

To reasonably self-advocate that you want more thinking time.

"I'm a visual processor. When could you send me that graphic?"

To help <u>them</u> learn how best to communicate with <u>you</u>.

★ RULE #8
LET GO

"The night of the fight, you may feel a slight sting. That's pride f***ing with you. f*** pride. Pride only hurts, it never helps." — Marcelus, Pulp Fiction

SOME DAYS...

Some days, it can feel like stresses, lies and horrible conversations are all your role entails. Horrible conversations can include ones about feedback, performance, troubleshooting, negotiating, or making plans. What makes them horrible is that we might hold a different point of view than everyone else, there might be someone in the meeting that we always clash with, or the topic and related decisions are causing us to compromise on our values to a large extent.

In the lead up to these kinds of conversations, we suffer poor sleep because of stress and anxiety — we're stuck in an endless loop of turmoil with no clear answers.

We feel stuck

You know, like anything we do every day, we come to accept the stress of being a leader as just part of our leadership responsibilities. And every day, we tolerate a bit more stress.

Our vagus nerve, our nervous system and our brain recalibrates all the time to accommodate and adjust to minute environmental changes, like our muscles adjusting our balance in milliseconds when we walk or run. Not something we notice.

We too easily acclimatise to new levels of stress.

But then we let rip

But then sometimes, the emotional charge is too much, our triggers stack up and we need to let some pressure escape, so we let rip. Even if it's not very graceful, it's a release.

We trade the risk of breaking trust and needing to repair our relationships and reputations, for the relief of truthfully expressing our frustration, our disagreement, or dislike... which could also be irrational, untrue, a miscalculation or misinterpretation, or even the result of our own lack of influence.

COULD OUR EGO BE PARTLY
TO BLAME?

Our need as leaders to have the answers, give people advice and tell our people what to do are the biggest reasons we feel stressed, we sometimes deceive ourselves, or lie to protect ourselves and others, going out of our way to avoid that horrible conversation.

We can thank our self-protecting, pride-filled ego for that.

I'm not saying that our ego is the only reason for the way we feel, but it is a large part of the issue. We have more choice over how we show up than we realise.

EVENTS THAT MAKE US WOBBLE

Stress escalates when we feel unsafe, need the approval of others or want to be more influential (among other things like burnout and lack of quality sleep). This includes when our direct reports don't do what we've asked, we feel out of our depth, our boss doesn't listen to us, or we need to have a horrible conversation.

Horrible conversations are loaded with emotions, illogical opinions, inexperience, bad memories, guilt, doubts and second-guesses as well as fear. That's why we avoid them.

LYING TO OURSELVES
IS A DEFENCE

Lying to ourselves works because it is a defence — it temporarily protects us and our team. Lying covers an amazing range of untruths and discomfort with reality from self-deception, avoidance, staying quiet, holding unrealistic expectations, polite pretence, and harmless little lies, to a blatant finger-pointing or career-damaging lie.

We all feel and do these things.

Skill and confidence in leadership — without stress, deception and a tendency towards conversation avoidance — is impossible if we don't first seek to understand what is happening for us and the other person.

WE *DO* HAVE CHOICES — WHAT WE LACK IS PRACTICE

What if I said, let go. Let go of your ego. What comes up for you?

And what if I said, you don't need to try so hard, that you don't need to have all the answers or the next steps. That you don't need to solve other people's problems.

I see it again and again in the leaders I train, though they don't see it as ego. Not at first. This strong attachment to their own counsel, their advice, their way of doing things. This is ego speaking. And it gets in the way of leadership.

All you have to do is put the person in front of you at the centre of the conversation. Listen deeply and ask questions.

✦ QUESTIONS & PHRASES ✦

"I have concerns about [...] Let me think on it.
Let's talk tomorrow."

To remove pressure from ourselves to respond immediately.

"Can we take a five-minute break?"

To decompress from a heated discussion and mentally reframe.

"Can you review the risks of each option,
and then let's revisit this?"

No heavy lifting on your part. Ask the other person to
refine the options.

"If you were making this decision,
what would you do?"

Offer them a chance to role-switch and put
themselves in your shoes.

"What's the impact if we don't do that?"

To sense-check the priority, urgency
or importance of something.

"Is there a third way?"

To surface an alternative approach that
satisfies more needs, better.

YOU DON'T NEED TO HAVE
ALL THE ANSWERS

You just need to be more present. Put your direct report (or boss!) at the centre of the conversation and solution creation. Help your people find their own answers and resist jumping in with your way of doing things.

How do you feel reading that? What might be possible for you? How could your stress levels be impacted? Would you still need to lie or deceive yourself? Would the conversation be so horrible?

As leaders, we can accept that stresses, lies and horrible conversations are all part of leadership. Or we can look for a healthier approach that uses coaching conversation skills and is better for us mentally and physically, that creates a healthier culture and team dynamic for our people.

Leaders I work with want to empower individuals to take ownership and responsibility, both because it is business critical and because they love seeing their direct reports work through challenges and reach their full potential.

No need to feel stuck in stresses, lies and horrible conversations.

In conversations, we have way more techniques and strategies at our disposal than we realise. Slowing down to notice, observe and adjust our role in them are just some of the things we can do to transform those stresses, lies and horrible conversations into rich exchanges with our direct reports, our peers, our clients and even our bosses.

★ RULE #9

NARCISSISTS ALWAYS WIN

"And she sat there for hours, not wanting to leave -
for the forest said nothing, it just let her breathe."
— Becky Hensley, Breathe

SORRY TO BREAK IT TO YOU

Working with ego-driven and narcissistic co-workers or bosses can damage us by killing our confidence. It's distressing, it messes with our heads and makes us doubt our own judgement. It also introduces risks into teams by creating silos, echo chambers, ethical blindness, discrimination, bullying and inequality.

And yes, it will make you angry. It's an important emotion that's telling you something noteworthy.

Let's explore what this mind-messing space looks and feels like.

BEING EGO-DRIVEN
OR NARCISSISTIC

Call it the shiny thing, the resonance of my own voice filling the airwaves and all eyes/likes on me, that flashy latest gadget that just happens to be mine, the best holiday I literally just came back from. I really love me. If you ever thought or hoped I might notice you, you are sorely mistaken, my adoring friend. It's not about you. It's about me!

Also, FYI... (you should be writing this down)... You need to do a whole bunch of work for me and not expect any appreciation or thanks for it. And when I'm telling people how great I am, I wouldn't risk pointing out that some other people actually helped me or that I have some details wrong. I'm on a roll, so don't interrupt my flow. Stay out of my way.

And definitely don't contradict me, because I will remember it and I will find a way to undermine you, deny you an opportunity, pick someone else to be on my team (someone who really adores me... until they start to see through me), rubbish you to your boss and the higher-ups, or, you know, point blank ignore you.

RECEIVING IT
AND GETTING SUCKED IN

Wow, such self-assurance. And everybody listens to you. Wish I could be like that. I'm going to stay close. If you're going places, then I want to be there. Even if I'm just on the side lines, or just a few sprinkles of your stardust land on me. What do you need doing? Hey, let me do that for you. It would be an honour. Oh wow, you had already picked me. Honoured x 2.

Hey, I saw this thing and I was thinking I could do... Oh, you want to do it? Okay, sure. Of course, no, really. I should have brought it straight to you in the first place. You'll do a better job of it than me anyway. You've got that shiny stuff going on. I'm happy to just help you celebrate it. If you mention me... no scratch that, forget I even thought about it. Shout if you need me.

RECEIVING IT AND GETTING EMOTIONALLY TRIGGERED

What am I missing? Everyone thinks you are totally cool. But you're a... I don't know. What are you? Everyone rates you but I'm not seeing it. Am I jealous? A little. Would I want to be you? Hell no. It would mean I'd have to be uncaring, self-absorbed, shouty. I'd have to constantly talk about how awesome I am, and make sure my boss sees no-one else except me when they've got that glitzy new role to fill.

So exhausting. I'm exhausted just being in your company. I'm exhausted thinking about the difficult conversations with you that I never get round to having. And you're not even any good at your job. Can I say that? You're incompetent. How can people not see that? The long hours I've worked fixing your s***... not even a 3 second mention. How do people like you exist? How do you keep rising through the ranks? What do I not get?

What am I doing wrong? Maybe I AM really jealous. No!! It's not that. But why do I feel so discombobulated? I feel disrespected. Powerless. And it's absolutely not how you should treat people. Why can't I let it go? Maybe it's me who's crap at my job. This keeps happening to me. Maybe I'm being too sensitive. Why should I care? It's just a job.

WITNESSING IT

Whoa... did that just happen? You literally took credit for all of THEIR work, in front of the whole team. And no-one is saying anything. Should I say something? Maybe it's just me. I imagined it. Oh no... you just did it again!! Seriously, is anyone else hearing this? You couldn't be farther from my personal values of integrity, respect, collaboration or [insert personal value] if you tried.

Oh, I am gutted for my teammate. They worked all weekend on that. They missed their mum's birthday to make sure our clients had what they needed for this week. I should have said something. I'm a rubbish teammate. I'm going to say something next time it happens.

What I really want to say is "You're a selfish, self-centred sorry excuse for a human being with not an ounce of empathy in your body." (Yeah, let it all out. Expletives allowed. No judgement here. You're angry and it's okay to feel angry at the injustice.) But I can't because that would mean lowering my own standards.

Okay, so now you're blanking me because I sent out a group note thanking my teammate. I see how it is. Well, maybe you'll change your attitude towards me once I get that... What? I'm not even being called for an interview?! But you are?! How the hell did that happen?

YOU'RE COPING, NOT THRIVING

I wish I could tell you there's a high chance these things are resolvable, but the stuff that makes narcissists uncoachable, also makes the chances of alignment, resolution or mediation... mmm, how can I put this... err... impossible. (I politely decline to coach leaders who display strong narcissistic traits.)

Drop it. You're never going to win. Not unless you've got Yoda on speed-dial.

Even if you teach yourself to respond differently, the reality is you are scaffolding yourself or your situation. You're coping, not thriving. The unjustness of what you experience and witness every day will cause you anxiety and upset.

If you're not in a position to influence a different outcome, you should seriously consider leaving that set-up if you value your wellbeing and happiness. While you have a narcissist in the mix, very little will change. And by the way, you have to ask why the higher-ups aren't doing anything about it.

HOW TO SURVIVE A NARCISSIST ✦

Stay and live with the mind-messing narcissist

Since they probably have a strong idea of what they want, conserve your energy and invite them to do the heavy lifting by asking,

> *"How would you like that to happen?"*

Some very grounded people approach it all with detachment as a people-watching sport with wonder in the human condition. But it can wear them down too in the end. If you find that not being able to offer your expertise presents an unacceptable risk, then consider the following options.

Move somewhere else in the company, another team or project

Find an influential ear and say,

> *"I would add more value to [...] team. How can we best explore that?"*

Ask for a different manager if your culture supports that option

Again, find a champion, and ask,

> *"How can I request you as my line manager? I can*

learn a lot from you."

Find somewhere better for you and then leave (in that order)

When you leave, be sure to thank your narcissist colleague or boss (because everyone has something to teach us) with,

"Thank you — I learned a lot working with you."

And breathe.

GUILT AND PERMISSION

And no, it's not you who is the problem. There are a lot of ego-driven and narcissistic people around. Sometimes you need to be to survive or make it to the top because the culture is such that this is what gets rewarded, no matter how progressive the organisation's policies are on paper.

The reality is a very different picture, and you have to decide if the fight is yours. It's probably not your fight and it's okay to say that. You have a lot to give. Somewhere else.

Whichever option you choose, have a strategy and timeframe for it happening so you feel more in control.

Guilt

Leaving does not mean you don't care about your teammates. It means you choose better for yourself. And you wish the same for them. But that is a decision they need to reach for themselves.

If they are good teammates, they won't hold it against you for leaving. You might even be sending them the strongest signal you can to give themselves permission to choose better.

Permission

It is more than 200% okay to want something better for yourself, just as you would want it for your teammate. But YOU have to give YOURSELF that permission FIRST before you can commit to leaving and do your **self-justice**.

I feel like I should tell you to be patient, try to reach an understanding with them, use your negotiation skills. And yes, it can work. A little bit. Maybe. But the truth is, in the end, you need to decide you've had enough, that you've tried, and it's time to choose better.

Choose wisely.

★ RULE #10

MODEL MEETINGS

"If a fact comes in that doesn't fit into your frame, you'll either not notice it, or ignore it, or ridicule it, or be puzzled by it — or attack it if it's threatening."
— George Lakoff

EMOTIONAL CONNECTIONS ARE *THE* POWERHOUSE

Working from home or remote working is going to continue and depending on which report you read, it's a good thing for work life balance (flexibility and productivity are up) or a bad thing for our mental health (stress levels and feeling isolated are also up). The reality is, managing our people remotely is harder and leaders may be underestimating how poor their emotional connections really are.

While the increased use of digital tools has meant we can continue with our jobs, we have found ourselves overwhelmed by those tools, feeling unproductive and inadequately supported by our bosses. So much so that 1 in 3 of us will be looking for a new job as soon as we can.

And there's also the fact that your remote work culture may be harbouring toxic behaviours, which are harder to locate when distributed electronically rather than physically experienced or observed.

Better spec kit, stronger internet connection, work time flexibility and a pay rise might fix the practical aspects of work, but what about feeling that our boss cares and knows how to be remotely supportive?

If we agree that the quality of our relationships is directly related to the quality of our conversations and time together, then our emotional connections could be the powerhouse of managing our people remotely.

So, how can we earn that emotional credit with our direct reports and people generally?

CONTRACT, CONTRACT, CONTRACT

When we feel complete trust and confidence in a member of our team to get stuff done with little oversight, it's likely we view them as highly competent or we have a strong emotional connection, or both. (Pst... they still need support and good conversations.)

When we worry that work might not be getting done and we give in to that irresistible urge to keep checking in, we've got some serious trust issues and a clear deficit in our emotional connection to that person. More on that in a moment.

Contracting is an important part of conversations where you both align on what needs to be done, by whom and by when. The bits that we don't do so well are:

- Clarifying what the consequences are of something happening and not happening

- Identifying what resources and help our direct report needs to successfully do the work

- Establishing how we will both know that progress is happening

- Agreeing how we will be both know the task is successfully completed

- Exploring what our options are should things not go to plan

Not only will this level of contracting bring both of you peace of mind and keep Big Brother at bay, but you as their manager will learn how your direct report thinks and you'll establish a better emotional connection.

OVERHAUL YOUR MEETINGS

We've taken a meeting model that works in the physical world and put it on steroids in the virtual world. We've been super-efficient and used morning and home commute times to squeeze in more meetings. Brilliant now we cover more time zones!

You don't need me to point out the heavy price we pay, physically and mentally, by extending our working days.

It's time to overhaul how we run our meetings.

Could you shorten your meetings to allow for five minutes of prep before and five minutes of reflection afterwards? Those who prepare for meetings swear it increases meeting output 2-3-fold. Plus, it's a good signal that you're working smarter, not harder.

Could you ditch a meeting and allocate that time to earning some emotional credit with your direct report? For example, have a quick pow-wow before a meeting to coach them on their contribution in the meeting as a growth opportunity for them.

And how about clarifying what your realistic working hours are? And when is it okay for folks to contact you about an issue while you're chillaxing? Being too available creates an unhealthy dependency on you. Not clarifying your availability means people will constantly breach your boundaries.

MAKE FEELINGS LESS AWKWARD

"You said that makes you [feeling]. Why is that?"

I get it — talking about feelings can be uncomfortable and awkward, especially if you're not a 'feelings' person. But in the context of a conversation between a leader and their direct report, this is a really, really important conversation skill to master.

When someone shares a feeling, they might be taking a big gamble. It's quite common to change the subject or even miss the cue entirely. But I promise you it's where the magic is, because if you can hold that space for them to talk it through, it might be all they need to push past something and find new energy.

Rambling, saying the same thing three different ways, contradicting ourselves and scratching our heads all count as talking it through. If that's happening, then you've got the secret potion to building strong emotional connections rich in oxytocin and other feel-good hormones. A.K.A. Emotional credit.

Emotional connections are the elixir that solve the unsolvable, bridge the widest gaps, and incentivise us to prioritise a task or goal higher just because we feel a bond with you. And it starts with just one really good conversation.

Banking emotional credit with each of your direct reports might even calm (or vanish) that stressful feeling in us of needing to see people working to believe they are really working or committed.

READ THE ROOM (OR SCREEN)

People are fascinating. The more we watch ourselves, the more fascinating we are. As a leader, people watching — in an observational (not creepy) way — is an essential skill because our truths play out in the combination of what we say and how we say it, both verbally and non-verbally.

Whether your meeting observations are virtual or in person, you can use them to coach your team members to get more intentional about their interactions for stronger conversation results.

What we say

Reading between the lines. When did you last do that?

Decisions are made so fast that we've come to take in only what someone communicates vocally or in an email or text, and we accept that to be true, factual or final.

Our choice of words, the phrases we repeat, the emphasis we place in our expressions, who we direct our words at as well as who we exclude, and the congruency (or not) with our body language, all tell us so much about what a person really believes and thinks. And who or what decision they are trying to influence.

It's not necessarily the case that they are trying to deceive us, it's more that they are not as aware of their own thinking or behaviour as we may assume. But, yes, sometimes they are trying to deceive us, and that's when people watching is incredibly valuable.

How we say it

Our mood, intention, inattention, self-awareness in the moment, who else is listening, our own emotional needs, our level of anxiety or confidence, and the energy of someone else all influence the intensity of or reduce what we are saying. How we say things reveals our real character and neuroses, the dynamics of our relationships and the strength of emotional connection with our teammates or stakeholders.

Whatever combination is at play can have us come off as ego-driven or ego-less, winging it or competent, uncommitted or passionate, as needy or very self-assured. And that can change from one environment to the next, which is why some people see us as confident and engaging while another group of people might have us down as quiet or unambitious.

Sometimes we don't say anything

Some of us don't want to say very much at all or will only speak to say something we feel is important and that hasn't been said or heard.

Some of us need time to reflect and think over the ideas and conversations we're listening to. We can need hours or days to go through our deep processing and analyse our thoughts and feelings.

And so, it never feels right to jump into a heated discussion or excited debate with an immediate reaction or our first thought. It might even feel scary.

And sometimes we want to be lied to

Yes, sometimes we want to be lied to because it serves our need to be liked, loved, admired, or even worshipped.

Also, we're more likely to accept a lie that confirms our own opinion or bias.

HOW TO PEOPLE WATCH
IN MEETINGS ✦

In Leaders Who Coach™, leaders learn to spot behaviours that they simply weren't aware of before. They discover that the trouble-spots were always in plain sight, they had just never registered them because they held opinions about people that weren't 100% true.

Here are some things to watch for in your next online or in person team meeting:

- Who interrupts, cuts across or speaks over other team members
- Who builds on what their team members have to say
- Who asks open questions that invite discussion
- Who asks closed questions that are in fact leading or loaded, or bating even!
- Who makes direct requests or asks for contributions or support, e.g.

"Given your experience, what do you think, Lizzie?"

- Who makes indirect, or soft asks, e.g. *"Some ideas from folks would be nice"* (and notice what response they do or don't get)
- Who doesn't say very much at all or stays quiet
- Who changes their body posture or facial expression in response to what someone is saying

Reflect on your observations, then line up one-to-one conversations with each of your team. Share your observations gently with,

"I noticed..."

and be ready to listen. Use the opportunity to explore how they can get more intentional about their interactions in useful ways to themselves and the team.

✦ QUESTIONS & PHRASES ✦

"What do you think is achievable in that time frame?"

To ensure plans are realistic.

"In your experience, what are we overlooking?"

To invite experienced, quieter team members to surface additional items.

"What concerns do we have?"

To invite dissenting points of view or resistance that members hesitate to express.

"What risks do we see with this approach?"

To invite team exploration on possible future blockers.

"What is a priority for us to address in this meeting?"

To give your meeting time a clear purpose.

"How can you monitor your progress?"

To align on timelines and expectations.

"You mentioned [feeling]. Can you say more about that?"

To grow their self-awareness about potential blockers.

"Something bothering you about that?"

When we sense some discomfort or hesitation.

WE'RE HARD WIRED TO CONNECT

We all get excited and sometimes we let our ego take over. And how other people behave can equally have a strong physiological and hormonal effect on us. It's all because of our desire to connect with people, to belong — it can whip up our emotions and lead us to find ways to synchronise with others emotionally and in our thinking.

All of this is why we're fascinating. All of this makes for great people watching. And as a leader, learning to observe can help us understand our people better, ask good questions, and be a consistent and balanced resource to our team members.

Connection is easier when we know our personal values and blind spots. Discover yours with our free Rulebook Mini-Course:

https://betterconversations.co/rulebook/#mini-course

KEEP EXPERIMENTING ✦

We mess up. Great! Keep going. Keep experimenting.

If one approach doesn't work, try out another one. There's beauty and honesty in messiness and imperfection. It's the joy of being human and having strong relationships.

Do less heavy-lifting

If we can't work it out, let's ask the other person:

> *"What should we talk about?"*

> *"How should we approach this?"*

Simplify

We over-engineer, over-complicate and then squirm about the details. There's relief in making an invitation and saying:

> *"I'm open to your ideas."*

Observe

Humans are funny creatures. Breathe. Watch. Learn. Appreciate. Enjoy. Breathe.

✦ ALL 88 QUESTIONS & PHRASES ✦

★ *Rule #1 — Earn Permission to Speak*

*"Would you like to hear
my position / thoughts on this?"*

"Why is that important?"

"You've mentioned [...] a few times.

What's significant about that?"

"What's brought you to that conclusion?"

"What have you thought about already?"

★ Rule #2 — Trust Underpins Reputation

"I love that you enjoy that!"

"I get how that's important to you."

"Your [value] is front-and centre on this one."

"I know the quality of [the work] is important to you, so help me understand what we cannot compromise on and what aspects we can negotiate on."

"Help me understand..."

"Let me know if you think I've misunderstood anything."

"In what way have I contributed to this situation?"

"I'm sorry, that wasn't my intention."

"How does the situation need to be different or better for you?"

"I'm hearing that this [event or way of being] is very important to you."

"How can I best support you with that?"

★ **Rule #3 — Zip It or Miss It**

"I appreciate you sharing that with me, thank you."

"How is it affecting you / your team?"

"How did that play out?"

"Your energy picked up / dropped off there... "

"I'm sensing... / I'm noticing..."

"What does [...] mean to you?"

"What makes you think that?"

"How does that influence how you see things?"

★ Rule #4 — Simple Questions

"Do you have an outcome in mind?"

"What might be another interpretation of what happened?"

"Where is the disconnect?"

"I wonder what was missed?"

"What's the worst that could happen?"

"What value does that provide?"

"What could be holding you back?"

"What do you think your options are?"

"Which of those would be good to explore further?"

"What needs to happen?"

"How can you test those ideas and assumptions?"

"What's coming up for you as you say that?"

"How is that significant?"

"Why does this decision need to be made now?"

"How true is that?"

"How can you confirm that?"

"What are you prepared to try?"

"How far can you take that idea?"

"How did you tell them?"

★ *Rule #6 — Less Haste, More Strategy*

"What are your thoughts on…?"

"What experience have you had with…?"

"Can I run something by you?"

"What's your position on this?"

"What concerns do you have?"

"What risks do you see?"

"What opportunities does this offer us?"

"Where would be a good place to start?"

"Who do you need to speak to and find out...?"

"What could go wrong?"

"What have we not thought of?"

"What would make this even better?"

"What do you need from me so you can do...?"

★ *Rule #7 — Put Second Impressions First*

"Hello, we haven't properly met yet. Can we grab a coffee?"

"Tell me more…"

"What does […] mean to you?"

"I understand this about […], is that your understanding?"

"What have your inputs been so far?"

"What might the consequences of that be?"

"I need time to consider this fully. Let's reconvene next week."

"I'm a visual processor. When could you send me that graphic?"

★ Rule #8 — Let Go

"I have concerns about […] Let me think on it.
Let's talk tomorrow."

"Can we take a five-minute break?"

"Can you review the risks of each option,
and then let's revisit this?"

"If you were making this decision,
what would you do?"

"What's the impact if we don't do that?"

"Is there a third way?"

★ *Rule #9 — Narcissists Always Win*

"How would you like that to happen?"

*"I would add more value to [...] team.
How can we best explore that?"*

*"How can I request you as my line manager?
I can learn a lot from you."*

"Thank you — I learned a lot working with you."

★ *Rule #10 — Model Meetings*

"Given your experience, what do you think, Lizzie?"

"I noticed..."

*"What do you think is achievable
in that time frame?"*

"In your experience, what are we overlooking?"

"What concerns do we have?"

"What risks do we see with this approach?"

"What is a priority for us to address in this meeting?"

"How can you monitor your progress?"

*"You mentioned [feeling]. Can you
say more about that?"*

"Something bothering you about that?"

★ **Keep experimenting**

"What should we talk about?"

"How should we approach this?"

"I'm open to your ideas."

✦

You will find a PDF of these 88 Rulebook Questions & Phrases in the resources section of our free Rulebook Mini-Course that accompanies this book, along with our Feedback Conversations Infographic detailing even more questions and phrases:

https://betterconversations.co/rulebook/#mini-course

Leaders Who Coach™ — The Course

Built on the principles of coaching mastery.
Infused with scientific & industry knowledge.

The next era in leadership practice, Leaders Who Coach™ puts powerful coaching skills into the minds and hearts of leaders responsible for unlocking their people's performance.

Leaders Who Coach™ is a truly "transformational" leadership learning experience that outperforms the majority of leadership development programmes because of its "richness", "clever layering of knowledge and practice" and opportunities for multiple mindset shifts from Day 1.

In just 4 months, leaders consistently report an increase in their self-awareness, confidence and capacity for empowering their direct reports by creating ownership, establishing accountability and holding difficult conversations.

With CPD accreditation, leaders and their organisations have a way of raising their coaching culture game, increasing tenure and loyalty, addressing mental health and performance flags early, and locking in change long term.

As well as tangible changes in the quality of their relationships and their ability to influence for good, graduating leaders express gratitude, relief, and renewed optimism for themselves and their teams to overcome challenges and achieve strategic business goals.

The Curriculum

Competency I — Grounded Leadership
Concept 1 — Managers vs Leaders vs Leaders Who Coach™
Skill #1 — Act with Integrity
Skill #2 — Establish Common Understanding

Competency II — Emotional Connections
Concept 2 — Trust-Permission Dynamic
Skill #3 — Build Trust, Secure Permission
Skill #4 — Coach-Leader Presence

Competency III — Conversation Skills
Concept 3 — The Who Energy Model™
Skill #5 — Listen to Understand
Skill #6 — Ask Good Questions
Skill #7 — Clean & Clear Language

Competency IV — Capability & Capacity of Teams
Concept 4 — The Growth Roadmap
Skill #8 — Grow Awareness
Skill #9 — Design & Agree Actions
Skill #10 — Plan & Set Growth Goals
Skill #11 — Accountability & Course-Correction
Skill #12 — Progress & Sustained Growth

Committed to delivering high quality leadership learning

experiences, Better Conversations & Associates Limited is a CPD
Member (Membership Number 13698) with The CPD
Certification Service (UK) since 2020.

For more insight into how we grow best as leaders, the four
competencies explainer videos, the article *Why Leaders Who
Coach™ creates transformation in leaders*, and much more at:

https://betterconversations.co/leaders-who-coach/

Leaders Who Coach™ — The Journeys

These are the words of Leaders Who Coach™ at the date of publication of The Rulebook. Hear more in-depth journey stories and video interviews using jump links at:

https://betterconversations.co/rulebook/#resources

"I'm such a lucky person to spend my time with clever and passionate people." — Mag Leahy, the 1st Graduate of Leaders Who Coach™ and now Head of Delivery and Tutor for Leaders Who Coach™

"Saying it was life-changing probably isn't an exaggeration." — Dan Dunton

"Leaders Who Coach™ has been a game-changer for me. It transformed the way I conduct meetings and 1-to-1 conversations. I wanted to feel much more confident that I have the tools to lead a conversation to long-term positive outcomes through a more human, empathetic approach — that telling someone to do something won't." — Troy Anthony

"I have truly enjoyed this course. The quality of the content, the practice in a safe environment, the stimulating conversation, the vulnerability has made it a great platform. I would recommend it highly." — Caroline Calvet Hurst

"Leaders Who Coach™ is great course for everyone interested in becoming a great leader and a better person. I gained a lot of awareness of myself, and valuable insights and methods to work with my direct reports and my teams." — Francisco Bertoni

"A mind-shift journey. I feel more grounded to support my teams with mindful, strategic conversations and decisions.

145

Each aspect of it feels intentional and all together immersive. It's awesome!" — Aisha Animashaun

"An incredible experience. Thoughtfully crafted to help you discover more about yourself and develop the skills necessary to become a great leader." — Muhammad Talib Uz

"I loved being on the Leaders Who Coach™ journey — it taught me so much about myself, my core values both professional and personally and what I can do to better support people I manage and work with. Overall, it has made me a calmer and more mindful individual, and given me the tools that will be beneficial for years to come." — Geraldine Goldie

"Insightful. A rewarding experience that sets the building blocks to develop yourself and your career." — Michael Sammin

"I'd always valued coaching conversations with others and found the most value from coming to my own conclusion. Leaders Who Coach™ has enabled me to feel more confident in providing that to others." — Sophie Johnson-George

"I would highly recommend this course. I have learnt so much about myself, others and the importance of showing up." — Danielle Main

"The LWC™ journey has been amazing. The lectures are insightful and practical. It made me aware of great possibilities in leading and coaching." — Nienke Gijsen

"If you're curious about coaching, passionate about growing people, and also pragmatic about the nature of coaching required as a people lead — I highly recommend LWC™." — Paul Bevan

"This course has given me tools to use in everyday circumstances, in and out of business situations. I feel more empowered as a coach to navigate my way through any

challenging people management scene." — Anita Dreosti

"The beauty of Leaders Who Coach™ is that it reveals your blind spots and develops you into a leader who can guide their team with Integrity, establishing Safe Environments, developing Connections and through great Communication to help them find issues and navigate them to find solutions, create plans, and follow up to track the progress with greater confidentiality." — Minakshi Bajaj Ashok

"I gained a lot of insight. At the start, I met complete strangers and was coaching them straight away. By the end of the course, they were all friendly faces and we had been able to experience each other's journey on becoming Leaders Who Coach™." — Andrew Richmond

"Everyone brings their style and flavour to a coaching conversation. Seeing others in the cohort in action was a fantastic way to learn and grow." — Valerie Dryden

"Leaders Who Coach™ felt like opening up a computer to find out how it's wired so you can operate it to its optimal point." — Terry Manyeh

"It's really an eye-opening experience. A journey alongside incredible people and led by wonderful tutors always ready to help and give." — Tanya Misheva

"Leaders Who Coach™ is brilliant, without exaggeration." — Eugene Yeskov

"I absolutely loved it. I learned so much and made some amazing connections with my cohort. Anyone thinking about developing themselves, just go for it!" — Laura Shrieves

"The single highest praise I can offer for anything is that it captures my interest, and makes me re-evaluate the world around me in a new way. Thank you all!" — Alison Lloyd

"It's a new way to lead and unlock the potential in your team. Honestly, it's transformational for me as a leader."
— Negar Farahmand

"Leaders Who Coach™ was excellent. Beautifully crafted with great thought and care, and it has been very inspirational." — Selina McCarthy

"Great course, great teacher." — Peter Hedley

"The Enrichment Calls were amazing, the tutors' knowledge of coaching is next-level and they are excellent facilitators." — Jayne Carmichael Norrie

"Provided me with a community of inspiring individuals that encourage me to learn and improve myself, and a strong set of skills to grow others." — Natalia Sharon

"Truly high-quality content, delivered superbly, and brought to life with the enrichment calls." — Uschi Baumann

"Has the theory, practice and feedback to help you on your journey. Couldn't recommend it highly enough. Feel privileged to have a supportive and inspiring group." — Robert Mackness

"A journey of learning and healing where I have reconciled the experiences of the past with the vision for my future. First class tutor. Empowering environment." — Glenn Martin

"I feel more confident in my conversation skills and awareness of how I can communicate with more clarity. Not only am I able to have more productive 1:1s but I am also able to coach my direct reports to be better people managers and leaders who coach themselves." — Åsa Nyström

"It was an amazing experience. I'm more patient in conversations and allow space for my team to show me how great they are. The BC team was amazing." — Tai Karun

"Paid back in multiples, improving my conversations and coaching abilities from the very first week. Come out more authentic, forgiving and curious." — Olwen Milne

"Exceeded my expectations. Feeling nourished and refreshed and gained the confidence to trust in my leadership and shake off what I thought "leadership" looks like." — Siobhan Baker

"Huge difference in the quality of outcomes through better conversations." — Kishor Patel

"Leaders Who Coach™ has really been an amazing experience." — Simona Sikorskyte

"The magical bridge between the past and the future I longed for. Leaders Who Coach™ helped me achieve that transformational alignment. I'm fully equipped to go into the future and succeed." — Evelyn Ebo

"Enormously beneficial in better understanding my team and their problems. Time to practice and develop these skills has given me the confidence to use them." — Steven King

"Loving it and cherishing every step of the way. I'm applying what we learn left and right." — Vera Trindade

"Such a wonderful course, which has improved both my coaching skills and my self-awareness, making me much more confident." — Claire Donald

"Hugely recommended!" — Ben Wilkins

"I've enjoyed learning about myself — generating a balanced and authentic leadership style that works with advocacy and content creation." — Carly Richmond

"A brilliant reminder for me that relationships are at the core of everything and experiential 'doing' is critical to

knowledge-building." — Donna Burgess

"I've gained skills that are benefiting me and my team right now, and will only continue to develop the more I practice. Can't wait!" — Laura McKechnie

"An opportunity to engage with leaders from different backgrounds and industries, a space to discuss, understand and appreciate everyone's experience." — Sîan Kinal

"I learned a lot from the Leaders Who Coach™ course and I am happy to recommend it to anyone interested in becoming a leader who chooses to coach." — Helen Scott

"Made me think about my leadership style and approaches in a different way. I really enjoyed the focus on empowering our teams for high-performance." — Kathryn Tingle

"Fantastic quality. I have grown as a leader and my team has noticed a difference in how I approach topics and questions. I really enjoyed the course." — Tom Hind

"Leaders Who Coach™ has been an inspiration to change my modus operandi with everything I do at work. It has encouraged me and built my confidence." — Paloma Aldeguer

"The skills that I have learnt in this course have not only accelerated my professional development, but have also enriched my personal relationships." — Eugenia Guerrero

"All of my conversations have improved as a result of being deliberate with my approach to being a better conversation partner. Thank you, Mag!" — Luke O'Mahoney

"Leaders Who Coach™ has helped me to listen more, ask the right questions and stop giving a solution for the problem." — Dorella Chu Rapizza

"I learned so much from watching and listening and have

noticed a change in my approach to conversations both professionally and personally." — Jess Hamilton

"My tutors, Mag and Uschi were capable of providing great insights on how to improve my coaching and leadership skills. Recommend!" — Çinar Yildirim

"I enjoyed everything: the assignments, the tutors, the resources provided — excellent course!" — Mariam Nersisyan

"Has touched every conversation I have had since starting the course." — Seb Millar

"I have gained a lot of practical skills and now have a much bigger toolbox to help my team and my organisation to tackle challenges and grow. Brilliant experience." — Snezh Halacheva

"I enjoyed how much I learnt about human behaviour and the new ways we can help people gain clarity. And meeting such lovely people." — Lizzie Daykin

"Coaching is a gateway for reflection on how your thoughts and behaviours influence your team. Through this course, I was constantly being exposed to my own projections and guided on how to remove them from my interactions to ensure a better result for my coachees." — Rukaya Adeyemi

"I enjoyed the sense of togetherness and the opportunity to see how others do things, to work to improve each other and ourselves." — Fraser Kettle

"I'm walking back into the world with a secret and powerful new awareness (a new superpower!). Utterly grateful. I feel more confident, clear, and effective." — Darcy Peters

"Finding what motivates people to go that extra mile and understanding where they see themselves in a few years, these are all very complex and nuanced things. Leaders Who Coach™ has taught me how to navigate them." — Victor Dewulf

"I can't recommend Leaders Who Coach™ enough." — Deborah Lewis

"This course is fantastic." — Sarah Gruneisen

"You have so much more power with the variety of questions that you can use and the tools and you are understanding how it is helping by actually practising it...the practical bit is really amazing. Now I understand people much better. I definitely recommend this course." — Richa Sharma

"Leaders Who Coach ™ was a life-changing experience for me in every avenue. I am putting into practice all the skills I have learnt. It has made me more aware of and in tune with my morals and values, which I align with daily. All that is left to say is Thank You to an amazing and supportive team!! Sehaam, Uschi and Mag — you ladies are truly amazing and inspiring!" — Heidi Cowie

Sehaam Cyrene PCC

Sehaam Cyrene is a leadership and team coach (PCC), founder of Better Conversations & Associates Limited (UK), creator of the **Coach-Culture Team™ Map**, and creator of CPD Certified course **Leaders Who Coach™**, delivered by an amazing team of accredited and international leadership coaches. A seasoned business leader, entrepreneur and live speaker, Sehaam is blazing a trail for coach-leadership and coaching cultures.

She also has a range of coach-leadership products for leaders, managers and teams at **TawKwrd.com**. Because there's more than one way to start a great conversation.

Based in the UK and of British and Libyan heritage, Sehaam is a single mum who is still learning to understand the neurodivergent threads in her children and is waiting to discover her own magic powers. Her personal values are Freedom, Integrity and Joy.

https://betterconversations.co/sehaam-cyrene/

LinkedIn: https://www.linkedin.com/in/sehaam/
Instagram: https://www.instagram.com/TawKwrd

BETTER CONVERSATIONS

https://betterconversations.co

My Coach-Leadership Journey

What have you discovered? What treasures of questions and phrases are you experimenting with? What are your personal values? How do you honour them? What are your blind spots? Where is the growth for you? Use these blank pages to capture your thoughts and reflections. Revisit them often. ❤

Printed in Poland
by Amazon Fulfillment
Poland Sp. z o.o., Wrocław

27172373R00096